I0820438

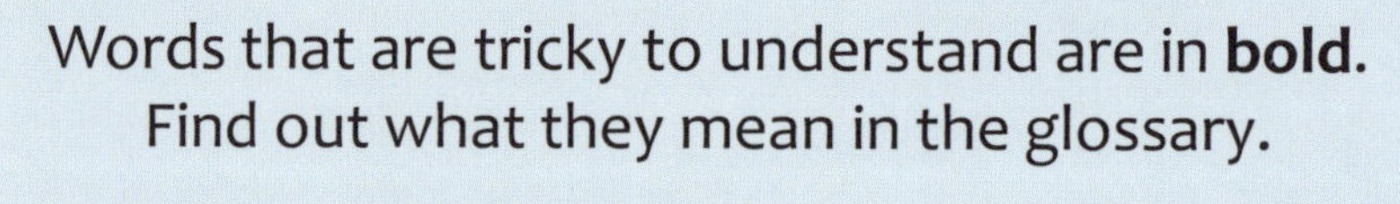

Words that are tricky to understand are in **bold**. Find out what they mean in the glossary.

Words that are difficult to say are in *italics*. Find out how to say them at the back of the book.

WHAT IS SEISMOLOGY?

Seismology is the study of **earthquakes**. It includes what causes earthquakes and the effects that they have on nearby areas.

The scientists who study seismology are called **SEISMOLOGISTS.**

COULD AN EARTHQUAKE SHAKE THE WHOLE WORLD?

DISCOVER THE SCIENCE BEHIND ***SEISMOLOGY***
(size-MOL-uh-jee)

Written by Rosie Rowntree
Illustrated by Denis Alonso

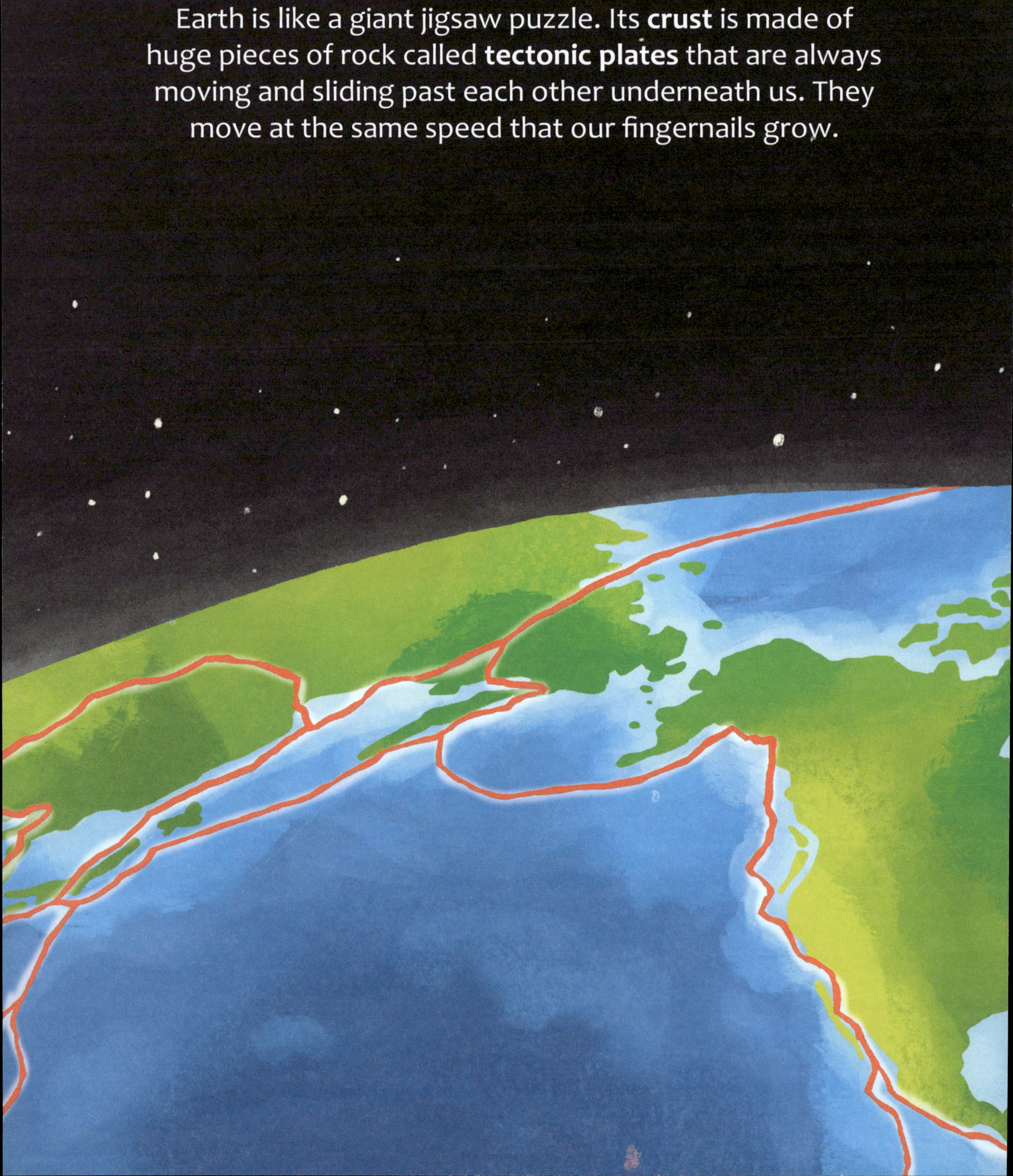

Earth is like a giant jigsaw puzzle. Its **crust** is made of huge pieces of rock called **tectonic plates** that are always moving and sliding past each other underneath us. They move at the same speed that our fingernails grow.

If one of these plates slips or breaks, it releases a lot of energy and **shakes the ground!**

We call this shaking an earthquake.

Scientists called *seismologists* use **seismographs** to detect the vibrations created by an earthquake and work out how strong it is.

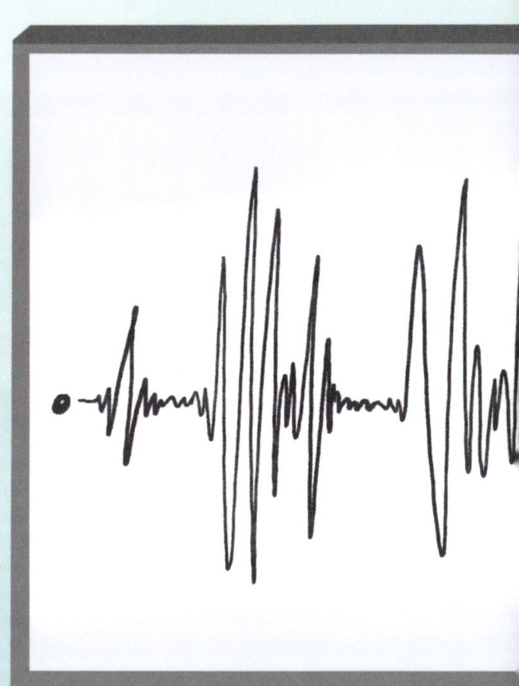

An earthquake's strength is measured in **magnitude.** If it has a magnitude of seven or higher, it can cause huge amounts of damage across very large areas.

In 2015, a magnitude 7.8 earthquake shook the Himalayan **mountains.** It was so strong that scientists believe Mount Everest – the tallest mountain on Earth – shrank as the ground beneath it dropped.

But this wasn't the largest earthquake ever – not at all!

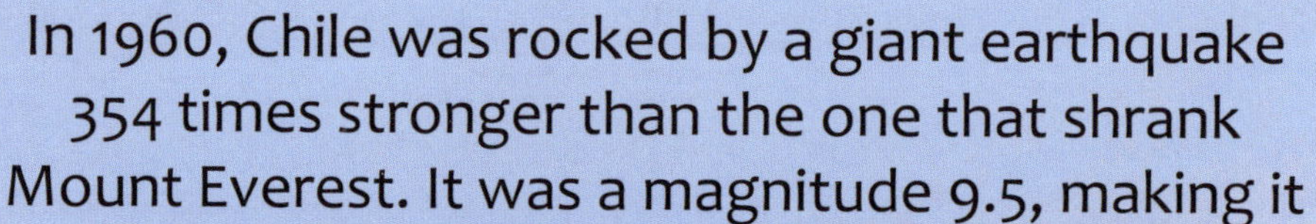

In 1960, Chile was rocked by a giant earthquake 354 times stronger than the one that shrank Mount Everest. It was a magnitude 9.5, making it

the strongest earthquake in human history!

In towns nearest to the middle of the earthquake, buildings collapsed and sadly many people lost their lives.

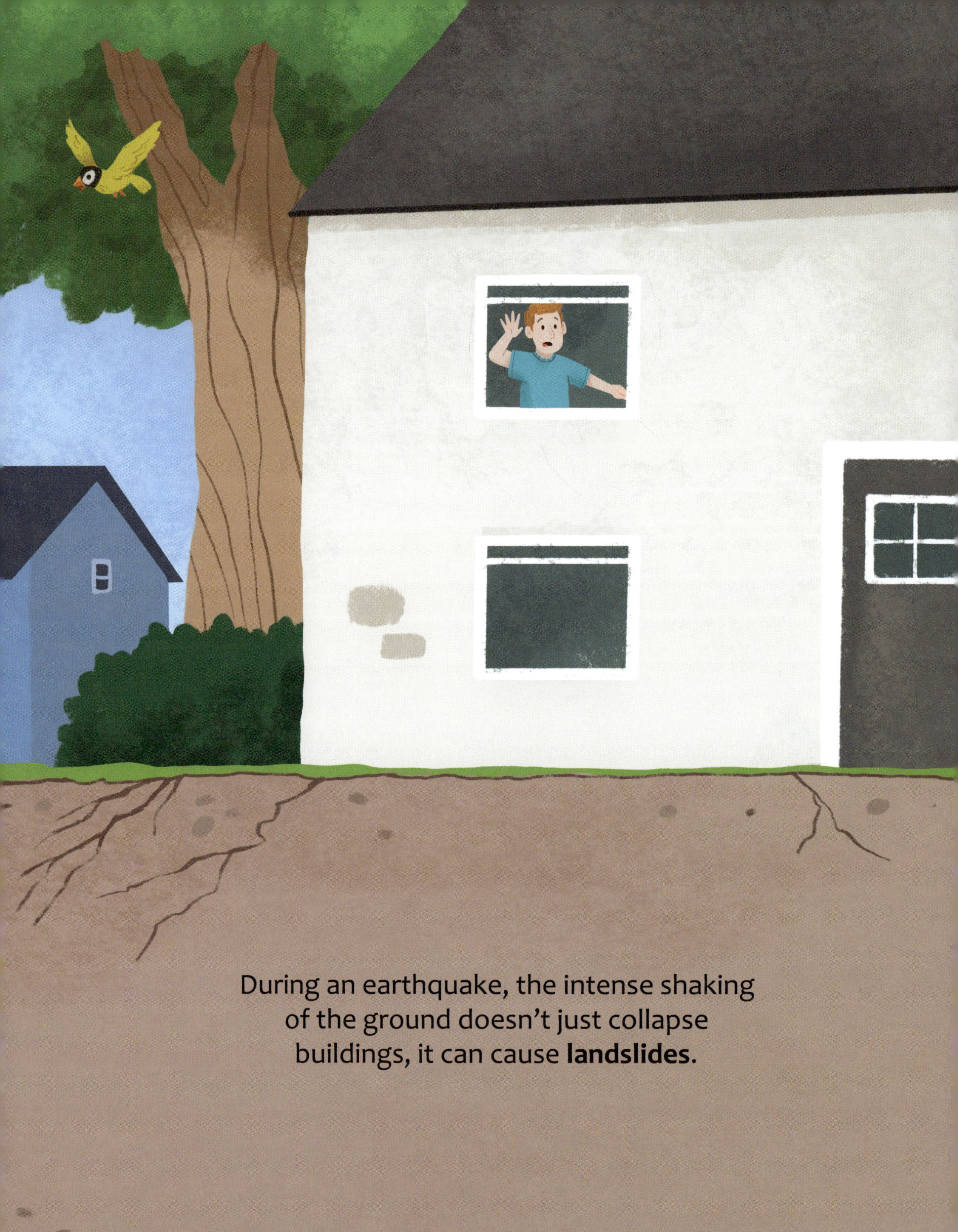

During an earthquake, the intense shaking of the ground doesn't just collapse buildings, it can cause **landslides.**

These dangerous **natural disasters** bury anything in their paths and can even leave houses hanging partially in the air!

Even after the ground has stopped moving, people still need to stay alert – especially if they live near the ocean. Earthquakes can also cause **tsunamis**!

Even though the 1960 earthquake was in Chile, a tsunami afterward caused lots of damage in Japan – which is over 10,000 miles (16,000 **km**) away on the other side of the Pacific Ocean!

The tsunami wasn't the only danger that people faced after the Chilean earthquake. Two days later, a nearby volcano that had been **dormant** for nearly 40 years erupted and sent clouds of **ash** flying 5 miles (8 km) into the air.

Scientists think that the volcano was already building toward an eruption, and that the earthquake gave it the final push it needed to explode – like a shaken soda can going pop!

The Chilean earthquake was a magnitude 9.5. Is it possible for an earthquake to reach a magnitude of 10 or higher?

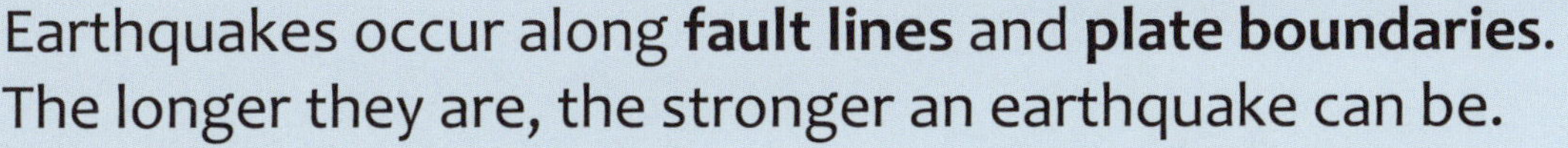

Earthquakes occur along **fault lines** and **plate boundaries**. The longer they are, the stronger an earthquake can be.

Thankfully, scientists don't think there is a fault line or plate boundary on Earth long enough to cause a magnitude 10 earthquake!

But that doesn't mean a magnitude 10 earthquake or higher is entirely impossible.

66 million years ago, an **asteroid** hit Earth. It wiped out the dinosaurs and caused an earthquake tens of thousands of times bigger than the one in Chile. Scientists think that it shook the whole world for days or even weeks!

Luckily for us, asteroid impacts as big as this one are very, very rare.

Seismologists can use information from previous earthquakes to **forecast** how likely it is for one to happen in a particular area in the future. However, they can't predict exactly when it will be.

But they are always looking out for signs. As soon as even the smallest **tremors** start, early warning sensors send out alerts. This gives people time – even if it's just a few seconds – to prepare themselves.

There are lots of ways that people can stay safe during – and after – an earthquake. This includes taking shelter under strong pieces of furniture, like desks.

In towns and cities next to the ocean, people move to higher ground after an earthquake in case of a tsunami.

In Japan, high-speed trains are automatically stopped to reduce the risk of them being shaken off their tracks.

It's not just people who need to be prepared for earthquakes. Buildings do too!

Buildings made of concrete used to be very stiff, and would break easily when shaken by an earthquake.

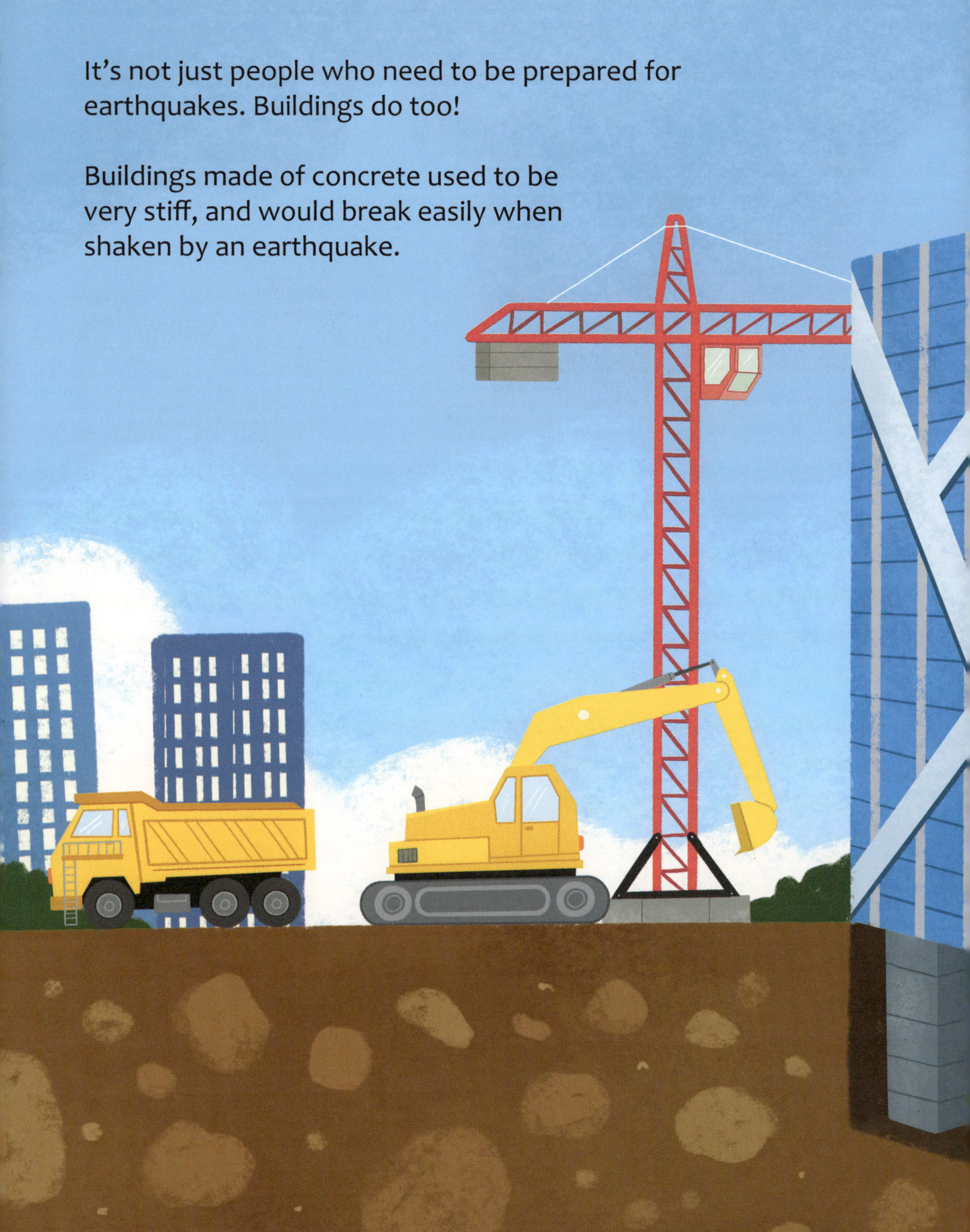

But now, with the help of seismologists, countries that experience many earthquakes are building **skyscrapers** that can **absorb** a lot of energy. They can bend and sway more without collapsing.

This makes them **a lot safer!**

As well as studying earthquakes on Earth, seismologists can also help to research other planets.

Earth isn't the only place that experiences **quakes**! Although they aren't caused by the same things as the ones on Earth, there are quakes on the Moon, Venus, and Mars!

Thankfully an earthquake strong enough to shake the whole world is very unlikely to happen – but it's still good to be prepared. Thanks to modern science, we know more about how to stay safe during an earthquake than ever before.

Record-breaking

NATURAL DISASTERS

Now that we know all about earthquakes, what other natural disasters does Earth experience, on land, at sea, and in the air?

CYCLONES

In 1996, **Cyclone** Olivia set the record for the highest recorded wind gust in a tropical cyclone. It was 253 mph (408 kph) – that's faster than most racing cars.

TSUNAMIS

In 1958, an earthquake in Alaska caused a landslide that dropped lots of rock into the ocean. It created the largest tsunami ever recorded, with waves reaching 1,720 feet (524 m) high!

LANDSLIDES

The largest landslide on the surface of Earth was 48 million years ago. Chunks of rock the size of mountains moved more than 25 miles (40 km)!

VOLCANIC ERUPTIONS

The eruption of Mount Tambora in 1815 was the biggest in human history. It created so much volcanic ash that it blocked out light from the Sun.

FLOODS

Scientists think that the largest flood on Earth was 5 million years ago. It was big enough to fill what is now the Mediterranean Sea!

Scientists are always working to monitor the planet to warn us of natural disasters before they happen, helping people stay safe.

Extraordinary

EARTHQUAKE FACTS

There's so much to discover about the world of seismology. Did you know these incredible facts about earthquakes?

WHAT ARE AFTERSHOCKS?

They are smaller tremors that happens in the days and weeks after a main earthquake, as Earth's crust readjusts. They may be smaller, but they can still cause lots of damage.

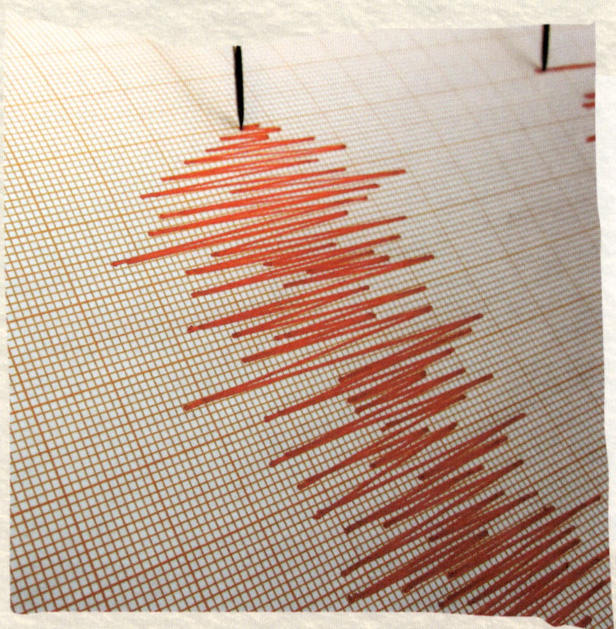

WHAT IS THE RICHTER SCALE?

It is a way of measuring magnitude. It was widely used, but now scientists prefer to use other scales that are more accurate – especially for larger earthquakes.

CAN EARTHQUAKES HAPPEN AWAY FROM PLATE BOUNDARIES?

Yes! However, these are rare and make up only 10% of all earthquakes. Scientists aren't entirely sure why they happen!

WHAT IS THE RING OF FIRE?

It is a horseshoe-shaped area around the edge of the Pacific Ocean where many tectonic plates meet. 80% of the world's earthquakes happen here.

CAN EARTHQUAKES AFFECT TIME?

In a way, yes! By causing Earth to spin slightly faster than normal, a magnitude 9.1 earthquake in Japan in 2011 shortened the length of a day by 1.8 **microseconds**!

GLOSSARY

Absorb – to soak up.

Ash (volcanic) – a powder that comes out of volcanoes during eruptions.

Asteroid – a space rock that orbits the Sun and occasionally falls to Earth's surface.

Crust – the solid outer layer of Earth.

Cyclone – a powerful storm that spins at high speed. *Need help saying this? Look below!*

Dormant – something that can go for a long time without any activity or growth.

Earthquakes – when parts of the ground shake. They can be very strong and destructive.

Fault lines – a long split between two blocks of rock.

Forecast – to predict or estimate something that will happen in the future.

Km – kilometers/kilometres.

Landslides – the sudden, fast movement of rock and earth down a slope.

Magnitude – a way of measuring the strength of an earthquake (see left).

Microseconds – units of time. There are one million microseconds in one second.

Mountains – rocky landforms that rise high above their surroundings.

Natural disasters – extreme natural events that can cause lots of damage.

Plate boundaries – the places where two or more tectonic plates (see right) meet.

Quakes – the shaking of a planet or moon's surface. On Earth these are called earthquakes (see left).

Seismographs – scientific instruments that can measure and record earthquakes (see left).

Skyscrapers – very tall buildings.

Tectonic plates – huge pieces of Earth's surface that move and can cause earthquakes (see left).

Tremors – a small shaking sensation. Tremors of the ground usually happen before an earthquake (see left).

Tsunamis – big sea waves, usually caused by an earthquake (see left) or volcanic eruption. *Need help saying this? Look below!*

HOW DO I SAY?

Cyclone
SY-klohn

Richter
RICK-ter

Seismologists
size-MOL-uh-jists

Seismology
size-MOL-uh-jee

Tsunamis
soo-NAH-me-z

THE BIG QUESTIONS ANSWERED

This is more than just a series of books; it is a complete resource. Accompanying each book is a variety of FREE material to engage curious kids with science.

www.thebigquestionsanswered.com

Use the QR code to visit the website, download free resources, and discover other books in the series.

On the website, find out incredible things about seismologists, including what they do, some of their greatest discoveries, and the people who have made a difference in this field of science.

The material is also available for home or classroom use, supporting all the information in this book.

Teachers' & Parents' Resources
With discussion prompts, questions, and extra information around key topics.

Activity Pack
Fun activities including creative writing, word searches, and more.

Audio Book
Experience this book in audio, narrated by a professional voice actor.

The Big Questions Answered is published by Beetle Books. Beetle Books is an imprint of Hungry Tomato Ltd.

First published in 2025 by Hungry Tomato Ltd
F15, Old Bakery Studios, Blewetts Wharf, Malpas Road, Truro, Cornwall, TR1 1QH, UK.

ISBN 9781835691502

A CIP catalog record for this book is available from the British Library.

With thanks to:
Editors: Jenny Rowan and Holly Thornton
Designers: Meg Holbrook and Amy Harvey
The team at Beehive Illustration
Consultant: Nicholas Mappin

Information in this book is up to date as of the time of writing.

Printed and bound in China.

Picture Credits:
(t = top, b = bottom, m = middle, l = left, r = right)